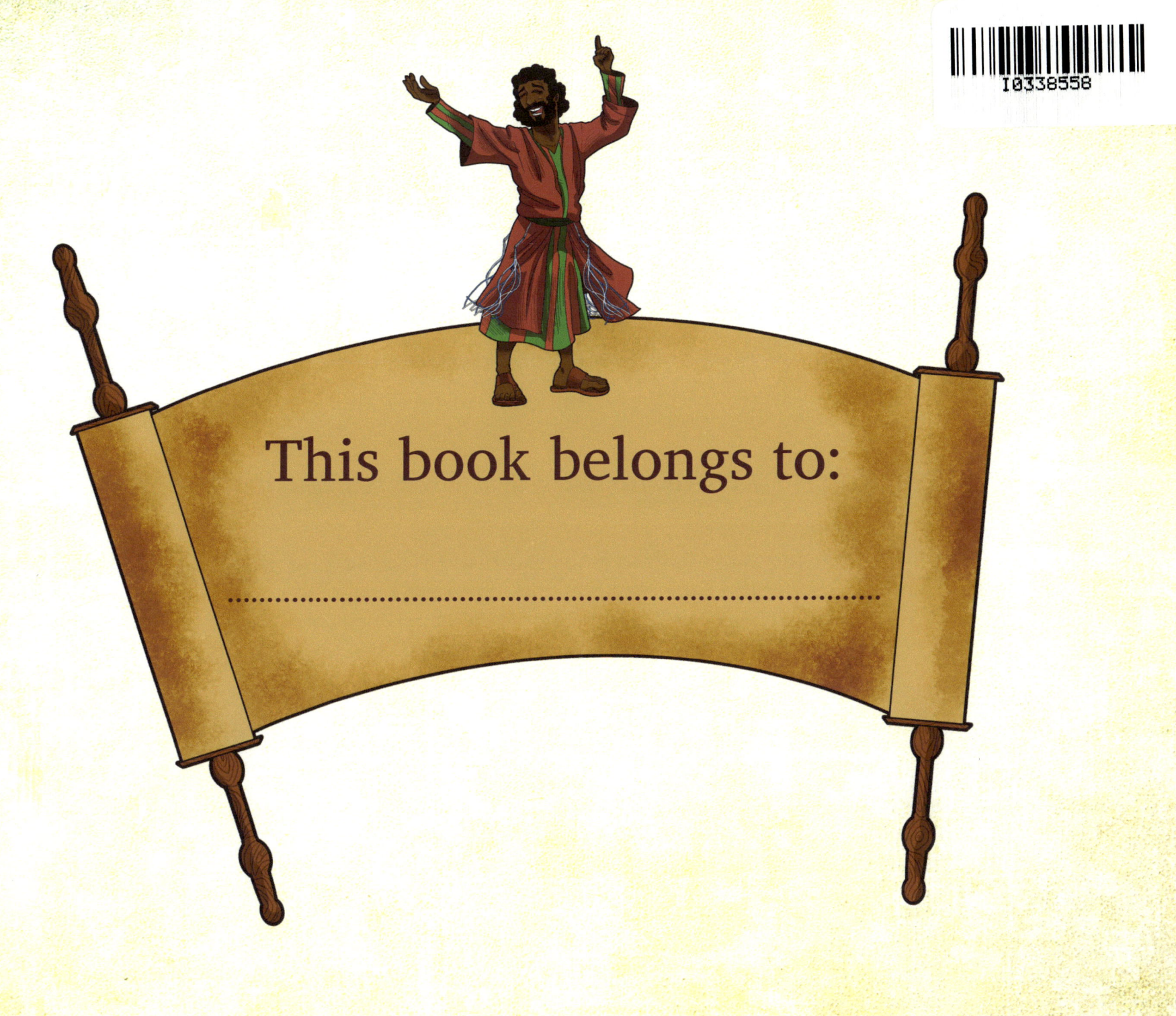

This book belongs to:

....

Copyright © BPA Publishing Ltd 2020

Author: Pip Reid
Illustrator: Thomas Barnett
Creative Director: Curtis Reid

www.biblepathwayadventures.com

Thank you for supporting Bible Pathway Adventures®. Our adventure series helps parents teach their children more about the Bible in a fun creative way. Designed for the whole family, Bible Pathway Adventures' mission is to help bring discipleship back into homes around the world. The search for truth is more fun than tradition!

The moral rights of author and illustrator have been asserted, this book is copyright.

ISBN: 978-0-473-41181-7

The Risen King

Death and Resurrection of the Messiah

"He is not here, for He has risen, just as He said" (Mat 28:6).

Pilate, the Roman governor, rose to his feet and faced the crowd. "Whom do you want me to set free?" he asked. "Barabbas, or Yeshua, the 'king of the Jews'?" Once a year the Roman governor freed a prisoner chosen by the people. "Crucify Yeshua!" the crowd shouted back.

Stirred up by religious leaders from the Temple, the crowd began to riot. Pilate had to act fast! "Take this man to Golgotha and crucify Him!" he thundered. The religious leaders smiled. They did not like how this teacher from Galilee spoke against their man-made rules and traditions. Their wicked plan to get rid of Him had worked!

The Roman soldiers placed a wooden beam on Yeshua's back and led Him through the city streets. The Feast of Unleavened Bread was about to begin and Jerusalem was filled with pilgrims. They pushed their way forward, eager to catch a glimpse of this famous teacher.

Beaten and weary, Yeshua fell to His knees and dropped the heavy wooden beam on the ground. The soldiers saw that He could go no further. They picked a man named Simon from out of the crowd and told him to carry the beam to Golgotha.

Judas bowed his head in grief. He had hoped with all his heart that Yeshua would be the one to overthrow the Romans. He did not understand the Scriptures that showed the Messiah would first come as a suffering servant. He had expected Him to come as a conquering king, like King David. "I have betrayed my Master," he cried. "He has done nothing wrong."

Grabbing the money the religious leaders had paid him, Judas hurried to the Temple. He burst into the courtyard and threw thirty silver coins on the ground. "I have sinned and betrayed an innocent man!" The religious leaders glanced at Judas, and then turned away. "This is your problem," they said. "You decided to betray Him!" Full of confusion, Judas fled from the Temple and killed himself in a field.

After Judas had left, the chief priests picked up the silver coins. "This is blood money," they stated, "and it is against our law to put it in the Temple treasury." They took the money and bought a field to use as a place to bury foreigners. It became known as the Potter's Field.

Did you know?

Jesus' Hebrew name is Yeshua. His full name is Yehoshua, which means, 'God is my Salvation'.

A large crowd followed Yeshua to a place just outside the city walls called Golgotha. Golgotha was where soldiers nailed people to a stake for disobeying the Roman rulers. This horrible punishment was known as crucifixion. Stripping off Yeshua's clothes, the Roman soldiers nailed His wrists to the wooden beam. Then they drove iron nails through His ankles to pin Him to a wooden stake. These two pieces of wood formed a cross.

Using ropes, the soldiers lifted the cross upright with Yeshua upon it until He was high off the ground. Beside Him they crucified a murderer and a robber, one on His right side and the other on His left. Above His head they placed a sign that said, "The King of the Jews."

Yeshua's enemies scowled at the sign. They did not believe He was the king of anyone. They went to Pilate and said, "Do not say He was the king of the Jews." But Pilate shook his head. He knew the religious leaders were jealous of this teacher from Galilee. "What I have written stays written," he told them.

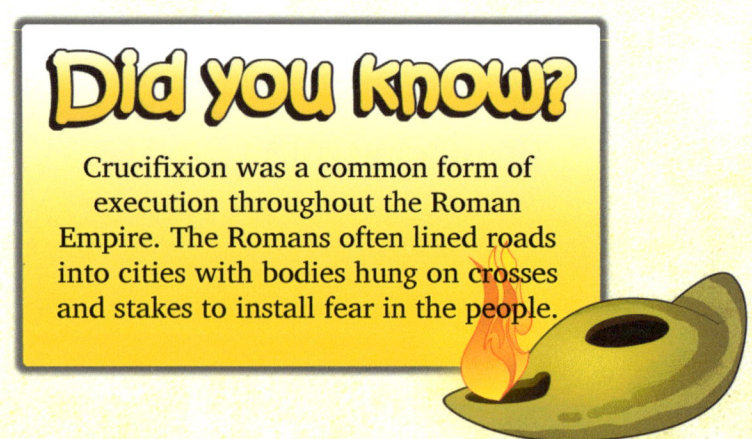

Did you know?

Crucifixion was a common form of execution throughout the Roman Empire. The Romans often lined roads into cities with bodies hung on crosses and stakes to install fear in the people.

That morning, people from near and far came to Jerusalem with their lambs for the Passover sacrifice. As they reached the city walls, many of them stopped and laughed at Yeshua. "You were going to destroy the Temple and rebuild it in three days," they said. "Come down from the cross if you are the Son of God."

Others stared at Yeshua in disbelief. They thought He had come to overthrow the Romans and become the king of Israel. But instead, He had been beaten and crucified. The people turned away and headed into the city, unable to look at the terrible sight.

The religious leaders came to mock Him, too. "He saved others, but He cannot save Himself. Let us see the king of Israel come down from the cross now!" The soldiers and robber insulted Him in the same way. "If you are the Messiah, save yourself and us." But the murderer defended Yeshua, saying, "He has done nothing wrong."

Even though His enemies made fun of Him, Yeshua still loved them and was willing to die for their sin. In great pain, He prayed, "Father, forgive them for they do not know what they are doing."

At midday a strange darkness fell over Jerusalem. For three hours the sun did not shine. At the Temple, priests blew the shofars to announce the start of the Passover sacrifices. The heavy gates swung open and thousands of people with lambs ready for slaughter poured into the Temple courts.

The Passover sacrifices continued at the Temple all afternoon. The priests sacrificed so many lambs that no one could count them all. Outside the city, Yeshua hung silently on the cross and did not say a word. While the soldiers waited for Him to die, they took His clothes and divided them among themselves.

All of a sudden, Yeshua cried out with a loud voice, *"Elohi! Elohi! L'mah sh'vaktani?"* which meant, "My God, My God, why have You forsaken Me?" Some of the people mocked Him saying, "Listen! He is calling for the prophet Elijah. Let's see if Elijah will bring Him down from the cross!" Sometime later, Yeshua said, "I am thirsty." A soldier offered Him a sponge soaked in sour wine to drink, but He refused to drink. Then He cried aloud, "My Father, into Your hands I place My spirit." He bowed His head and died.

Around Jerusalem, strange and mysterious things began to happen. A huge earthquake shook the city. Rocks split open and the earth around the cross cracked like an egg. The special curtain in the Temple ripped from top to bottom. This curtain separated an inner room called the Holy of Holies from the rest of the Temple. Only the high priest could go behind the curtain once a year.

At Golgotha, a Roman officer standing guard marveled at everything that had happened. "Truly this was the Son of God," he said. Not far away stood Yeshua's friends and family, including his mother Mary, Mary Magdalene, and other women who had followed Him from Galilee. They stared up at the cross, weeping and mourning for their Master.

The soldiers guarding the cross had one more job to do. They broke the legs of the murderer and thief in order to speed up their deaths. But when they came to Yeshua, they saw that He was already dead and did not break His legs. Instead, one of the soldiers plunged a spear into His side. Blood and water poured out of His body. It splashed onto the ground and ran through the crack in the earth.

That afternoon, a secret disciple of Yeshua named Joseph hurried to see the Roman governor. Joseph was a member of the Jewish religious council called the Sanhedrin. He had not agreed with their decision to have this man put to death. Plucking up courage, Joseph asked Pilate for the body of Yeshua. Pilate was surprised to hear that He had already died. "Is this true?" he asked his soldiers. "Crucified men usually take much longer to die." When Pilate heard that it was so, he ordered the body to be taken down from the cross and given to Joseph.

With the help of his friend Nicodemus, Joseph carefully wrapped the body with a white linen cloth and placed it in his own new tomb cut out of solid rock. Opposite the tomb, the women who had come from Galilee watched to see where Yeshua's body was placed. Then they hurried into the city to prepare spices and perfume for His body.

Just before the sun began to set, Joseph and Nicodemus rolled a large stone in front of the tomb so no one could go in or out. At the same time, the sky over Jerusalem filled with smoke from ovens roasting thousands of Passover lambs. People gathered to eat the lamb and to remember how God had helped their ancestors escape from slavery in Egypt.

The next day, several religious leaders hurried to see Pilate. Even though Yeshua had died, they were afraid His disciples might steal His body. "This man said He would rise again," they told Pilate. "Give us soldiers to guard the tomb in case His disciples steal His body and tell everyone that He has risen from the dead."

Pilate sat on the edge of his seat and drummed his fingers. He did not want Yeshua's disciples causing trouble during the Feast of Unleavened Bread. "Go and guard the tomb," he told his soldiers. "Make it as secure as you know how."

The Roman soldiers marched to the tomb and hammered an iron spike into the rock so the door could not be rolled open. Then they watched the tomb all day and all night so no one could come and steal the body away.

Did you know?

Rich men were buried in their own tombs, often cut out of solid rock outside the city. Yeshua's burial in this tomb fulfilled Isaiah 53:9 that said, "And they made his grave with the wicked, and with the rich in his death…"

Three days after Yeshua died, another huge earthquake shook Jerusalem. A bright light flashed around the tomb, and a fearsome angel in shining white clothes dropped from the sky like a thunderbolt.

The soldiers guarding the tomb were terrified. They fell on the ground as if they were dead. They were no match for the risen King and His mighty angel. At the same time, many ancient tombs broke open outside the city. Holy men who had died were raised to life and came out of their tombs.

When the soldiers woke up, the angel had disappeared. The stone door had been rolled away and the tomb was empty! They raced into the city to tell the religious leaders what had happened. But the religious leaders were busy. It was the Day of First Fruits, an Appointed Time where people thanked God for the coming harvest. On this day each year, the High Priest waved the first part of the barley harvest before God at the Temple. The nervous soldiers stood outside and waited for the ceremony to finish.

"An angel moved away the stone door," the soldiers told the religious leaders when they finally met. "The tomb is empty. We don't know where the body has gone." A chief priest raised his hand to silence the men. He did not believe in angels or life after death. "We cannot tell people the body is missing. They might believe this man was the promised Messiah and come after us."

The religious leaders agreed. They did not want Yeshua's followers to riot during First Fruits. Instead, they came up with a cunning plan. Handing the soldiers a large bag of money, they said, "Say that His disciples came in the night and stole His body while you slept."

The soldiers looked at each other anxiously. They weren't sure if they liked this idea very much. In the Roman army, soldiers who fell asleep on guard duty were put to death. "Do not worry," added the religious leaders. "If Pilate hears what happened, we will protect you."

Did you know?

Many people believe there are different ways to pronounce God's name. These include Yah, Yahweh, Yahuah, and many others.

Afraid the religious leaders would arrest them, too, the disciples hid inside a house in Jerusalem where they could not be seen. The men prayed and wept for their Master who had died. Even though He had explained many times about His coming death and resurrection, they still did not understand.

All of a sudden, Mary Magdalene burst through the door. Gasping for breath, she cried, "I have seen the Messiah!" That morning she had gone to the tomb with spices to take care of His body. But to her amazement, the stone was already rolled away and the tomb was empty.

She had run to tell the disciples, but only Peter and John had gone with her back to the garden. They had seen the empty tomb, but they had not seen Yeshua. Now Mary had come back with this news. "A man who was a stranger approached me," she said. "I thought He was the gardener, but it was our Messiah!"

Before she could finish speaking, the rest of the women arrived at the house. Earlier that morning they had gone to the tomb and seen two angels. The women all started to talk at once, comparing stories about what they had seen. "Yeshua wants you to go to Galilee," Mary Magdalene told the disciples. "He will see you there."

That same day, two disciples left Jerusalem for a village called Emmaus. As they walked along the road, the men talked about all the strange and amazing things that had happened during the Feast.

A stranger soon joined them on the road. "Why are you sad?" He asked. The disciples stopped. "Have you not heard about the death of the great teacher Yeshua? He taught many people about God's Kingdom. We believed He would set us free from our Roman rulers, but the religious leaders demanded that He be put to death."

The stranger shook His head. "You foolish ones. It is written in the Scriptures that the Messiah will die for His people's sin." Then using the words of Moses and the prophets, He explained how and why the Messiah had to die. The disciple's hearts filled with joy.

When they reached Emmaus, the two disciples invited the stranger in for a meal. As He blessed the food, they recognized that the stranger was Yeshua. But in an instant, He disappeared. The disciples nearly jumped out of their skin with excitement! They raced back to Jerusalem to tell the other disciples that Yeshua had risen from the dead.

Back in Jerusalem, the two disciples told the others about the risen Messiah. "We spoke with the Master! He explained the Scriptures that say He is the Savior of Israel." The other men nodded. "It is true. Peter also saw Him while you were away!"

While the disciples talked about the Scriptures, Yeshua suddenly appeared amongst them. *"Shalom Aleichem,"* he said. "May peace be upon you." The disciples' mouths dropped open. In front of them stood the Master. "He must be a ghost!" they cried. "All the doors and windows are locked. How else did He get inside the room?"

Yeshua smiled at His frightened disciples. "Don't be afraid. Come closer and touch Me." He showed them the scars on His wrists and ankles. "See, I am not a ghost. I have flesh and bones." The disciples reached out and gently touched His scarred wrists and side. "You truly are the Son of God," they said.

News of Yeshua's resurrection spread quickly throughout Jerusalem. Not even His own brother James had believed He was the Messiah. Now he and many others finally believed.

Peter and the disciples left Jerusalem and traveled to Galilee. It was springtime and the hills were filled with flowers and birds. They passed camels carrying goods from Egypt and merchants with grain for Rome.

One evening while the disciples waited for Yeshua, they went fishing on the Sea of Galilee. Even though they fished all night, they did not catch even a single fish. As the sun rose the next morning, they spied a stranger standing on the shore. They did not recognize that the stranger was Yeshua.

Yeshua called out to them, saying, "Throw your net on the right side of the boat." When the disciples did what He said, the net became so full of fish that their small boat almost sank. "Look!" John pointed to the stranger. "It is the Messiah!" Throwing on his robe, Peter jumped out of the boat and swam quickly toward the shore. John and the disciples followed in the boat, dragging the net full of fish behind them. They were all excited to see their Master again.

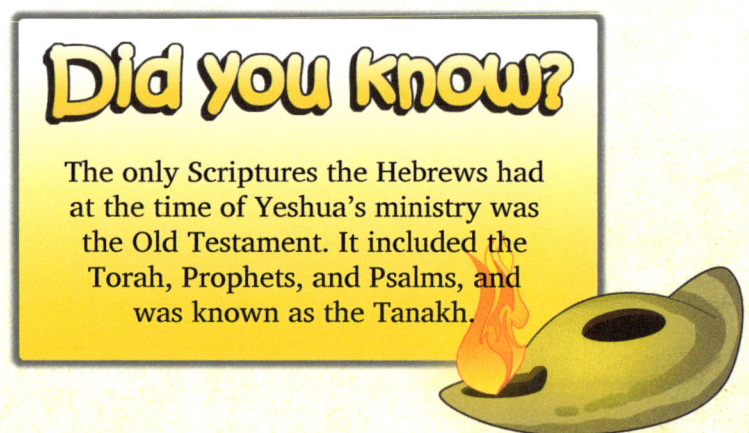

Did you know?

The only Scriptures the Hebrews had at the time of Yeshua's ministry was the Old Testament. It included the Torah, Prophets, and Psalms, and was known as the Tanakh.

When the disciples reached the shore, they saw a fire with fish on it and bread. "Bring some of the fish you have just caught," said Yeshua. Their stomachs grumbling, the hungry disciples handed Him fish from their net. None of them dared ask Him, "Who are you?" They knew in their hearts it was their risen king.

That morning the disciples sat on the shore and ate a delicious breakfast of fresh fish and bread. After they had eaten, Yeshua turned to Peter. "Do you love Me?" he asked him three times. Peter looked at the ground. He still felt ashamed that he had denied knowing the Messiah. "Yes, you know that I love you," he said each time. "Then feed My sheep," said Yeshua. He wanted Peter to care for and teach His people, Israel.

The Messiah appeared to His disciples many times after He rose from the dead. He talked with them again and again about the Kingdom of God and explained how the Scriptures all pointed to Him. And He gave them important instructions. "Go everywhere and make disciples. Teach them to do everything that I have taught you," He said.

Peter and the disciples left Galilee and set out for Jerusalem to celebrate the Feast of Shavuot. The road was crowded with people and oxen carrying baskets of grain to the Temple. Everyone sang and danced, and praised God for this special thanksgiving Feast.

In Jerusalem Yeshua appeared to the disciples one last time. He ate with them, saying, "Stay here in the city and wait for God's Holy Spirit." Afterward, He led them out to the Mount of Olives where He raised His hands and blessed them. Then without another word, He rose into the sky before their very eyes, and disappeared out of sight.

The disciples were amazed. Where had their king gone? As they peered into the sky, two men dressed in white suddenly appeared beside them. "You Galileans! Why are you standing here looking at the sky? One day your king will come back in the same way you saw Him go up to Heaven," they said.

The disciples returned to Jerusalem full of joy. One day they would see their Messiah again! But for now it was time to begin their mission to which Yeshua had sent them - to spread the Good News of the risen King and His love for His people everywhere.

THE END

TEST YOUR KNOWLEDGE!

(Match the question with the answer at the bottom of the page)

QUESTIONS

Who sentenced Yeshua to die on the stake? ....

Who carried Yeshua's crossbeam to Golgotha? ....

Which of Yeshua's disciples betrayed Him? ....

Who rolled away the tomb stone? ....

Yeshua rose from the grave on which Appointed Time? ....

What did the Roman soldier use to pierce Yeshua's side? ....

Who asked Pilate for Yeshua's body? ....

Who met two disciples on the road to Emmaus? ....

After the resurrection, where did the disciples go fishing? ....

What important instructions did Yeshua give His disciples? ....

ANSWERS

1. Pilate, the Roman Governor
2. Simon
3. Judas
4. An angel
5. Day of First Fruits
6. A spear
7. Joseph of Arimathea
8. Yeshua
9. Sea of Galilee
10. Go and make disciples

Complete the Word Search Puzzle

DISCIPLES
GALILEE
JUDAS
PASSOVER
PILATE
GOLGOTHA
MESSIAH
TEMPLE
ROMANS
TOMB

```
P R V G Y P Q M D O
I A O Q I N C T I G
L L S M K M L J S O
A D I S A A S U C L
T O M B O N A D I G
E O E Z M V S A P O
J G U P T R E S L T
M E S S I A H R E H
G A L I L E E N S A
D Z T E M P L E F B
```

Bible Pathway Adventures®

Birth of the King
Betrayal of the King
Swallowed by a Fish
The Chosen Bride
Saved by a Donkey
Thrown to the Lions
Facing the Giant
Witch of Endor
Sold into Slavery
The Great Flood
Shipwrecked!
The Exodus
Escape from Egypt

Discover more Bible Pathway Adventures' Bible stories!

Check out Bible Pathway Adventures Activity Books

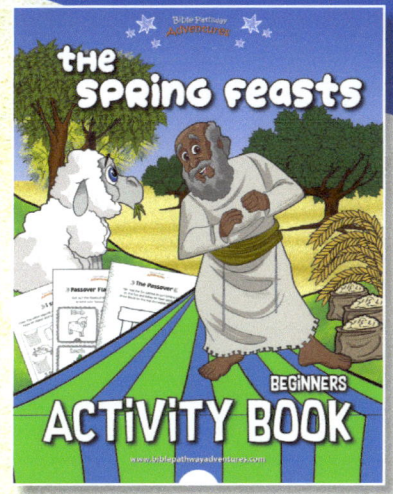  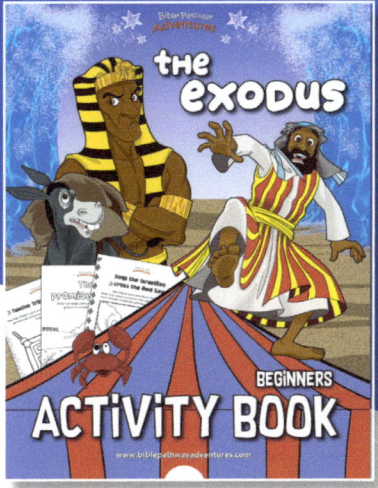 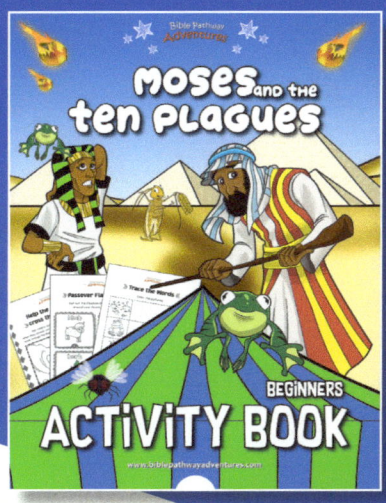

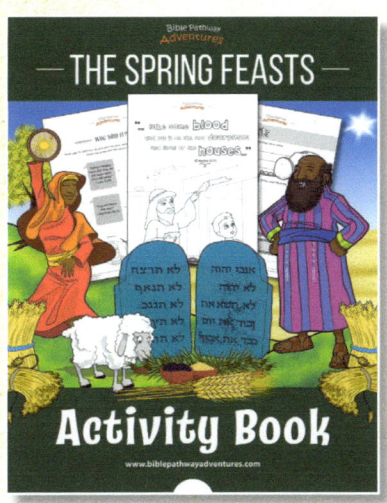  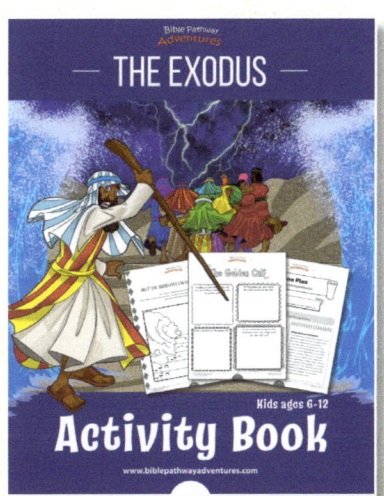 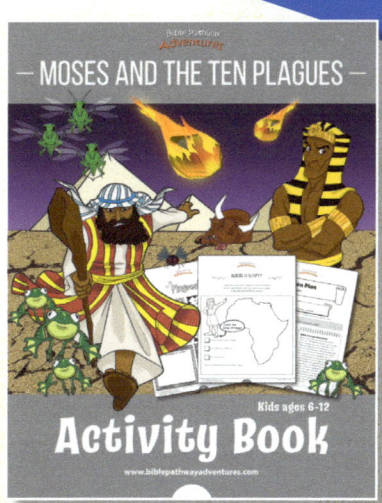

GO TO

www.biblepathwayadventures.com

www.ingramcontent.com/pod-product-compliance
Lightning Source LLC
Chambersburg PA
CBHW041323290426
44108CB00004B/117